This
Yuletide Journal
Belongs To:

_____

December 22nd – Northern Hemisphere
June 21st – Southern Hemisphere

Thanks for buying this journal!
I have lots more available on Amazon, including:

- Journals
- Undated Planners
- Composition Books (for school)
- Holiday themes
- Mermaids, Seahorses, starfish (I live near the beach, constant theme!)
- Florals & botanicals
- Hobby-themed journals for gardening, yoga, chakra-balancing, and other self-improvement topics – and some witchy stuff!

I'm Wanda, and Moon Magic Soul is my brand – welcome to my tribe!

Visit me:

www.moonmagicsoul.com

www.facebook.com/moonmagisoul

Using this Journal/Workbook

Welcome to the Season of Yuletide and the Winter Solstice!

The pages are a way for you to explore and celebrate the season – to document your thoughts and feelings about Yule, and also to reflect on the past year, and plan for the new year!

Fill out what speaks to you – what you'd like to express. Ignore what doesn't fire you or interest you.

The first few pages are some month and week pages for personal planning. There are two months and six weeks – which gets you from Samhain and past Yule. If you already have a personal planner, you can art journal or ignore those pages.

Journaling – there are lots of journal prompts, have some fun with it! There are also some blank pages for you to doodle, scrapbook (paste or glue things) or make plans without lined pages.

Blessed be!

Thursday	Friday	Saturday

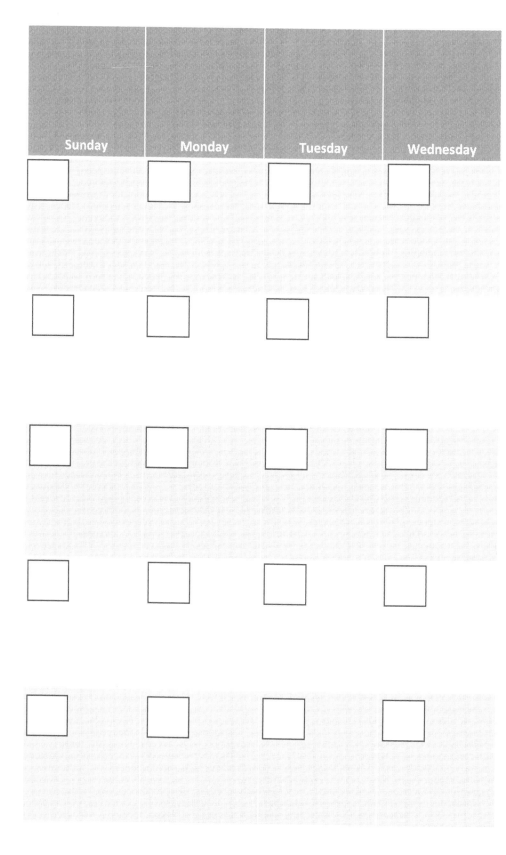

MONTH

Thursday	Friday	Saturday

_____

Monday

Tuesday

Wednesday

Thursday

Saturday

Sunday

Notes

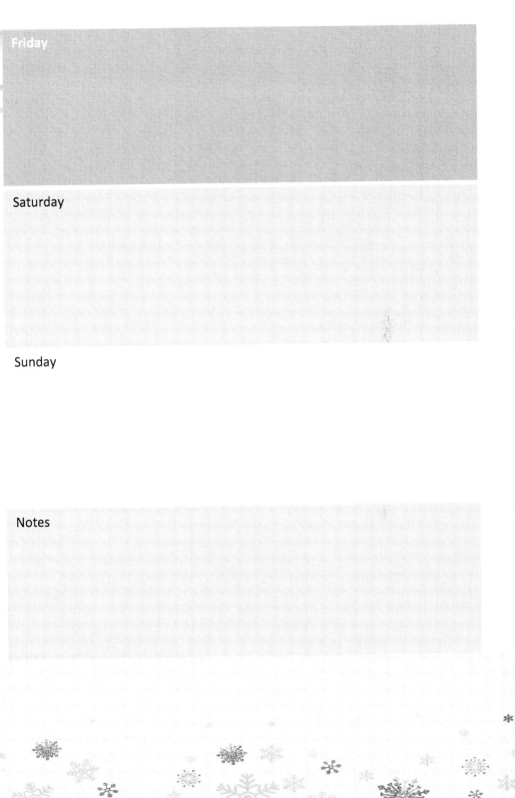

WEEK OF:

_____

Monday

Tuesday

Wednesday

Thursday

Friday

Saturday

Sunday

Notes

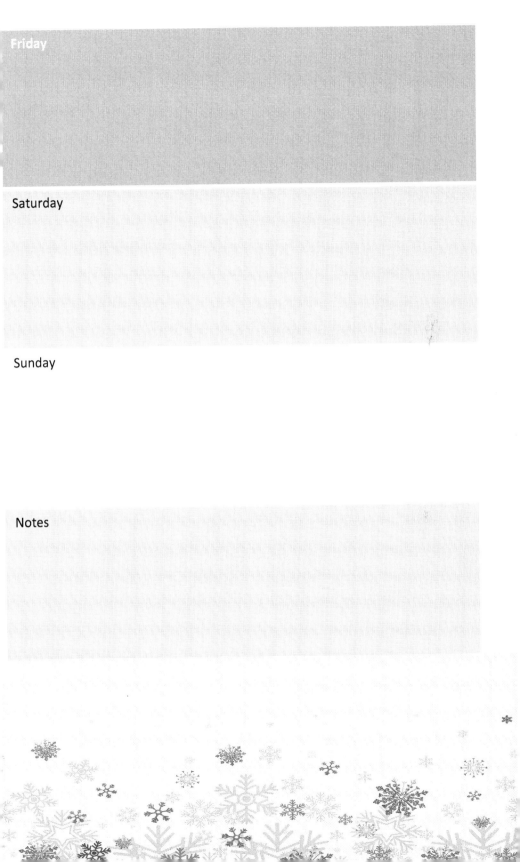

_____

Monday

Tuesday

Wednesday

Thursday

Saturday

Sunday

Notes

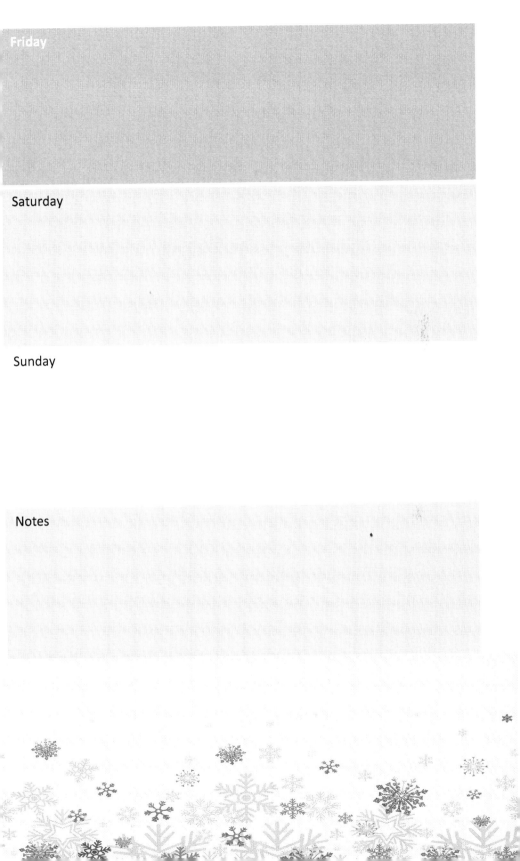

WEEK OF:

_____

Monday

Tuesday

Wednesday

Thursday

Friday

Saturday

Sunday

Notes

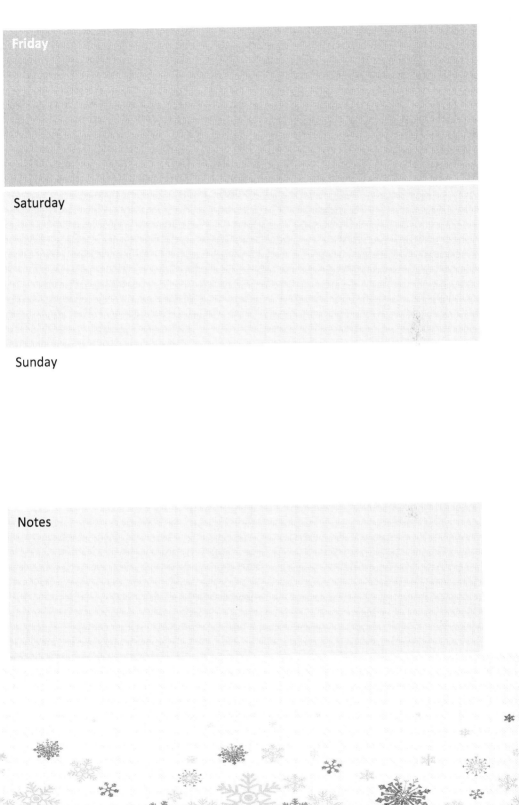

WEEK OF:

_____

Monday

Tuesday

Wednesday

Thursday

Friday

Saturday

Sunday

Notes

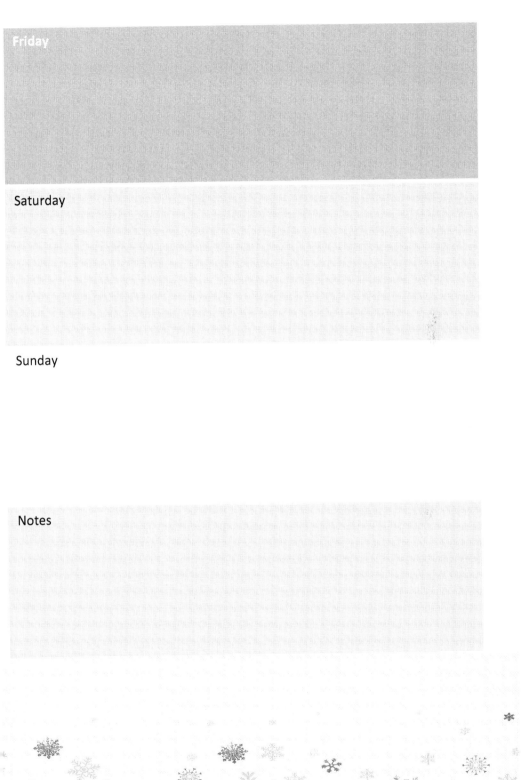

_____

Monday

Tuesday

Wednesday

Thursday

Friday

Saturday

Sunday

Notes

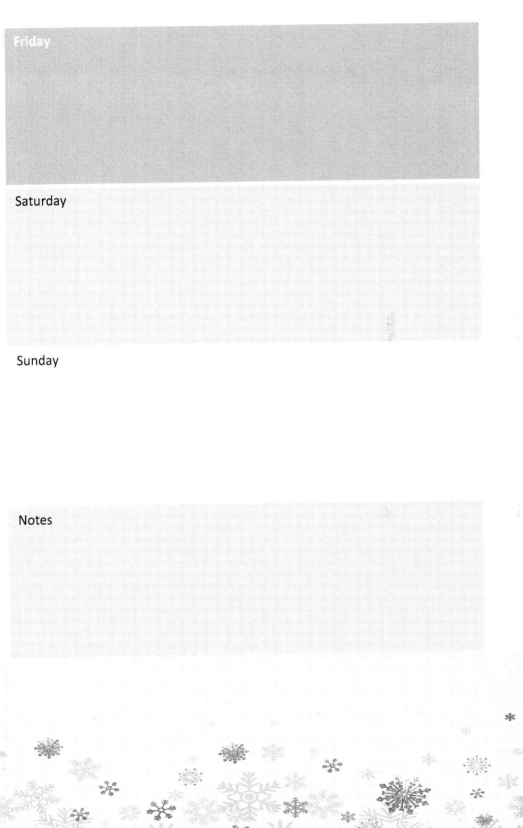

Meaning & Keywords

- ❏ Birth of the New Year
- ❏ Settling into and enjoying the cooler/cold weather
- ❏ Inviting the light into your home and into your life
- ❏ Exchanging gifts with friends and family
- ❏ Gifts to charitable organizations
- ❏ New beginnings and change

How have you celebrated the past few months of autumn?

_____

_____

_____

_____

_____

_____

_____

_____

_____

_____

_____

_____

_____

_____

_____

_____

_____

_____

How has your life changed since last Yuletide?

How do you feel about the cooler weather?

How do you plan to bring the light into your life?

_____

_____

_____

_____

_____

_____

_____

_____

_____

_____

_____

_____

_____

_____

_____

_____

_____

_____

Do you have plans for exchanging gifts with friends and family this year?

_____

_____

_____

_____

_____

_____

_____

_____

_____

_____

_____

_____

_____

_____

_____

_____

_____

_____

What charitable organizations are you donating to this year?

_____

_____

_____

_____

_____

_____

_____

_____

_____

_____

_____

_____

_____

_____

_____

_____

_____

_____

_____

_____

What are you ready to let go of?

What are you ready to manifest in your life?

Scents of the Season

- ☐ Cinnamon
- ☐ Pine
- ☐ Rosemary
- ☐ Sage
- ☐ Wintergreen
- ☐ Oranges
- ☐ Peppermint

Scenting Your Home

- ☐ Incense
- ☐ Candles
- ☐ Essential Oils with Scent Sticks
- ☐ Essential Oils in Diffusers
- ☐ Essential Oils rubbed on air vents
- ☐ Commercial plugs-ins (no judgment!)

What scents make you think of winter?

How do you plan to use scent this season?

_____

_____

_____

_____

_____

_____

_____

_____

_____

_____

_____

_____

_____

_____

_____

_____

_____

_____

_____

Decorations

- [ ] Colors – Gold, green, red and white
- [ ] Candles & bonfires
- [ ] Yule logs
- [ ] Reflective paper
- [ ] Sparkly glass decorations
- [ ] Strings of lights
- [ ] Evergreen trees, swags and wreaths

Do you decorate the entrance to your home to welcome the birth of the new year?

_____

_____

_____

Do you decorate the living space of your home for winter?

_____

_____

_____

What decorations are you seeing when you go out?

_____

_____

_____

_____

_____

_____

_____

_____

_____

_____

_____

_____

_____

_____

_____

_____

_____

Foods

- [ ] Nuts
- [ ] Potatoes & Root Vegetables
- [ ] Apples
- [ ] Squashes
- [ ] Smoked Meats
- [ ] Highly spiced breads, cakes & cookies
- [ ] Eggnog, wassail, mulled wine, warmed drinks

Do you celebrate the seasonal foods with special treats like gingerbread and fruit cake?

_____

_____

_____

Do you enjoy warmed seasonal drinks with family and friends?

_____

_____

_____

Do you bake cookies with your family and friends?

_____

How will you celebrate Yuletide with food and drink?

Activities for Yuletide

- ❑ Set up your altar – use gold, green, red and white!
- ❑ Have a potluck dinner with family and friends (share your food stores!)
- ❑ Exchange gifts with friends and family
- ❑ Make donations to charity
- ❑ Sing songs together
- ❑ Donate your time by volunteering!
- ❑ Start a new positive habit
- ❑ Let go of a negative habit or belief

What items are you using to decorate your altar?

How often do you re-decorate your altar?

Sketch a new plan for your altar setup here:

What gifts are you giving this season?

_____

_____

_____

_____

_____

_____

_____

_____

_____

_____

_____

_____

_____

_____

_____

_____

_____

_____

_____

How can you volunteer your time this season?

What songs do you like to sing with friends and family?

_____

_____

_____

_____

_____

_____

_____

_____

_____

_____

_____

_____

_____

_____

_____

_____

_____

_____

_____

_____

_____

_____

Habits to Start…

What bad habits and negative beliefs are you ready to let go of?

_____

_____

_____

_____

_____

_____

_____

_____

_____

_____

_____

_____

_____

_____

_____

_____

_____

_____

_____

_____

_____

_____

_____

_____

Ideas...

- [ ] Drive around and look at holiday light displays.
- [ ] Make it a point to greet the sun one morning.
- [ ] Enjoy the beauty of a sunset one evening.
- [ ] String lights outside and inside your home!
- [ ] Light a salt lamp at night at the front of your home to invite light into your home.
- [ ] Drape garlands of greenery with ribbon entwined over a doorway or on a tabletop.

How are you planning to celebrate the winter solstice season?

_____

_____

_____

_____

_____

_____

_____

_____

_____

_____

_____

_____

_____

_____

_____

_____

_____

_____

Spell Work & Rituals:

- ☐ Sun magic – inviting the light of the sun into your practice lightens up the darker days
- ☐ Honor the birth of the new year (the sun god)
- ☐ Use tarot cards, runes, scrying or other divinatory tools to seek guidance about the new year; write a summary of your process and any messages received
- ☐ World peace & world healing
- ☐ Happiness, hope & unconditional love
- ☐ Manifesting of change and new beginnings - Write down your bad habits on a piece of paper and burn them, setting the intention that you're going to replace them with good habits

How will you incorporate sunlight into your magical practice?

_____

_____

_____

_____

_____

_____

_____

_____

_____

_____

_____

_____

_____

_____

_____

_____

_____

_____

_____

How will you honor the birth of the new year?

_____

_____

_____

_____

_____

_____

_____

_____

_____

_____

_____

_____

_____

_____

_____

_____

_____

_____

_____

_____

What divination tools will you try this season?

What will you work through to initiate change and new beginnings this season?

_____

_____

_____

_____

_____

_____

_____

_____

_____

_____

_____

_____

_____

_____

_____

_____

_____

_____

_____

_____

_____

Joining your voice with others can cause powerful action. How will you work for world peace and world healing?

_____

_____

_____

_____

_____

_____

_____

_____

_____

_____

_____

_____

_____

_____

_____

_____

Are you desiring of happiness, hope and unconditional love? What spell work can help with these desires?

_____

_____

_____

_____

_____

_____

_____

_____

_____

_____

_____

_____

_____

_____

_____

_____

_____

_____

_____

What bad habits are you ready to release for the new year?

What are your favorite divination tools? Why?

_____

_____

_____

_____

_____

_____

_____

_____

_____

_____

_____

_____

_____

_____

_____

_____

_____

_____

_____

_____

_____

_____

Divination –
Looking Forward:

The next pages are spaces for you to record by month what your favorite divination tools are telling you about your upcoming year.

Make it a habit to review your reading on a monthly basis, and make comments about what has unfolded. Leave space in between for future journaling and exploration!

Month 1
The Season of Winter

Month 1
Reflections

_____

_____

_____

_____

_____

_____

_____

_____

_____

_____

_____

_____

_____

_____

_____

_____

_____

_____

Month 2
The Season of Imbolc

Month 2
Reflections

Month 3
The Season of Spring

Month 3
Reflections

_____

_____

_____

_____

_____

_____

_____

_____

_____

_____

_____

_____

_____

_____

_____

_____

_____

_____

Month 4
The Season of Ostara

Month 4
Reflections

Month 5
The Season of Beltane

Month 5
Reflections

Month 6
The Season of Litha

Month 6
Reflections

Month 7
The Season of Summer

Month 7
Reflections

Month 8
The Season of Lammas

Month 8
Reflections

Month 9
The Season of Late Summer

Month 9
Reflections

_____

_____

_____

_____

_____

_____

_____

_____

_____

_____

_____

_____

_____

_____

_____

_____

_____

_____

Month 10
The Season of Samhain

Month 10
Reflections

Month 11
The Year Begins

Month 11
Reflections

_____

_____

_____

_____

_____

_____

_____

_____

_____

_____

_____

_____

_____

_____

_____

_____

_____

Month 12
The Season of Yule

Month 12
Reflections

Yule

Samhain

Imbolc

21st December

1st November

1st February

Winter Solstice

Spring Begins

New Year

Christmas

St. Brigid's Day

Halloween

Mabon

Ostara

21st September

Autumn Equinox

Easter

21st March

Michaelmas

Spring Equinox

May Day

Lammas

St. John's Night

May Day

Lughnasadh

First Harvest

Summer Solstice

1st May

1st August

21st June

Beltane

Litha

Thanks for buying this journal!
I have lots more available on Amazon, including:

- Journals
- Undated Planners
- Composition Books (for school)
- Holiday themes
- Mermaids, Seahorses, starfish (I live near the beach, constant theme!)
- Florals & botanicals
- Hobby-themed journals for gardening, yoga, chakra-balancing, and other self-improvement topics – and some witchy stuff!

I'm Wanda, and Moon Magic Soul is my brand – welcome to my tribe!

Visit me:

www.moonmagicsoul.com

www.facebook.com/moonmagisoul

Made in the USA
Middletown, DE
23 November 2023